"*The Humble Warrior* si  ll
that men are capable of .... it
has been dominated by .... s
a new freedom and recl .... ,
intuition, heart-connect .... e
await you within the pages of *The Humble Warrior*. So, take a deep
breath. Then take another. Open your heart, stay curious and enjoy
the journey!"

— Jonathan Ellerby PHD

"In a culture obsessed with outward appearances and never-ending
quests for more material satisfaction, I love Chris' approach to
spiritual fitness. *The Humble Warrior* is the perfect blueprint to attain
balance – both physically and spiritually. His wisdom serves as true
nourishment for those who are starving for a more meaningful and
harmonious existence."

—Jason Wrobel, Celebrity Vegan Chef and Author of "Eaternity"

"The most valuable thing any one of us has is our story. Chris does a
masterful job of sharing his in *The Humble Warrior*, as well as showing
readers how to connect more deeply with their own greatness. As one
of his mentors, it's inspiring to see how committed he is to leading
and helping others transform their lives."

—Bo Eason, Athlete, Speaker, Performer, Author

"*The Humble Warrior* offers a deeply intimate and fresh approach to
experience profound transformation by listening to the HEART!
Chris' practices are powerful, and anyone can do them."

—Jonny Kest, Center For Yoga

"*The Humble Warrior* provides the tools to connect to our highest
energy and performance. This book provides hope and guidance, so
that you can have a life full of meaning, impact, and connection".

—Joel Kahn, MD, Clinical Professor of Medicine

Edge.

Thank you for the support. Blessed & Grateful to have a friend like you.

Live Brave

Cfart

The Humble Warrior

Spiritual tools
for living a
purposeful life

CHRIS FORTE

To my three daughters:
Ava, Brooke, and Simone

"Your life is a journey. Your pain and suffering are not a random coincidence; they will lead you to your higher purpose. Listen to your heart, because the resources for you to fulfill your purpose are inside of you. Yes, your treasure lies within you…and God is always with you."
— *Chris Forte*

Contents

Part 2: Principles of a Humble Warrior: Spiritual Fitness Tools

Part 3: Spiritual Fitness Writing Exercises

Introduction

Right now, you are reading this book for a reason. God, the Universe, your Higher Self – whatever your belief system – wants you to experience the wisdom within these pages or to give "The Humble Warrior" to someone in your life who could use it.

"The Humble Warrior" is an enlightened, daily practice for men. It is intended to enable you to slow down, look within, handle the obstacles in your life with grace, and ultimately, live a more purposeful life. I call this practice of inner contemplation and review, "Spiritual Fitness". For over 30 years, I've completed this practice consistently every day and the rewards continue to astound. I've healed the deep pain in my life, and I can see an ever-unfolding clear path before me.

It is my hope, that in reading "The Humble Warrior", you choose to apply the seven easy daily practices I am about to share with you, so that you, too, can develop a life of solid discipline, commitment and devotion that will propel you to transcend your personal pain and suffering and fulfill your life's greater purpose.

††

The Origin of "The Humble Warrior" Book

On December 25, 2014, a Voice commanded me to write. *Write what?* I started writing, stream of consciousness style, and my pen wrote by itself: "Book, radio show, website, blog…"

I didn't have any idea what the message meant, but it sparked an urge in me to lay my journals of the past 17 years out on the bed. However, since I didn't yet know what to write – or even how to start – I left them lying there and headed to a yoga class.

As I moved through the various postures at the class, my teacher, Jane, said, "Go into the Humble Warrior position." So, I lay down on my right side and planted my forearms and third eye solidly against the ground. As soon as my bowed head touched the hard surface of the floor, tears suddenly gushed down my cheeks. My wife and I had filed for divorce a month earlier. There it was – the death of my marriage. The floodgates opened.

Lying on the floor, I now understood why the pose was called, The Humble Warrior, because I was filled with a deep sense of reverence and humility.

As the yoga flow continued, I then shifted onto my left side. This time, when my forearms and third eye touched the ground, I felt love, compassion, forgiveness, and kindness, as if a beaming smile had just poured itself directly into my heart.

The last position of the class was called, "Shivasana". I lay in stillness on my back, shut my eyes, and observed my breathing return to a relaxed state. I inhaled deeply, and immediately heard a beautiful Voice say, "You now have the name of your book, radio show, and your blog. Call it 'The Humble Warrior.' Go forth and do this to heal, grow, and share."

✝✝

In the first part of the book, I will share my personal story. You will learn about the experiences that led me to directly hear "the Voice", which I now know to be God at work in my life. I offer "The Humble Warrior" to you from my heart in the hopes that by sharing my story, you (or someone you love) will be uplifted. I hope that my story plants some seeds of faith in you for overcoming the obstacles you encounter in your life.

In the second part of the book, I share the "Principles of a Humble Warrior" and my "Spiritual Fitness Tools" that will help you to align with your best life. As a former Division I athlete, current yogi, and Spiritual Entrepreneur, I originally came up with the term "Spiritual Fitness" to align both worlds – to create the ultimate body, mind and spirit workout. This practice will help you to discover your greater Truth and highest Love, even in the midst of challenging circumstances.

✝✝

Got God?

It's extremely important to me to try to be as neutral and balanced about the word "God" as possible. Please substitute the term that is most significant and meaningful to you as read "The Humble Warrior" – "Universe," "Krishna," "Goddess," "Jesus," "Buddha," "Kuan Yin," "Mohammed," "Mother Mary," "Great Spirit," "Yeshua," "Almighty," "Higher Power…"

✝✝

I discovered it was only possible for me to overcome the difficult obstacles in my life by first developing a relationship with God. The Spiritual Fitness practices I've created became the daily key for me to develop this profound relationship, even with the busyness of my life.

I realize you might operate on overdrive as much as I do. I offer my Spiritual Fitness Tools to all of my brothers, so that you can reconnect to God, even in the midst of your very busy life.

Through discipline and devoted practice, I've learned my life purpose—to love others, to love myself, to stay in loving action, and to share what I have learned about loving myself with others.

When we love ourselves and commit to loving others, we can share our infinite light with the world – we are the light. Although we cannot avoid pain, we can make choices and create changes in our lives. We can put an end to harming ourselves and others.

The story you are about to read is about freedom – finding it, seeking it, losing it, and finding it again. Through baseball, weight lifting, gambling and partying; through money, entrepreneurship, living the "American Dream", and hitting rock bottom; through running, swimming, divorce, weight training, yoga, and in diving deep into spirituality – a "Humble Warrior" is born.

Many blessings on your journey. Live Brave.

PART 1

The Voice

CHAPTER 1

Freedom is Both a Feeling and a Voice

The first time I heard "the Voice," I was 12 years old.

I woke up one Saturday morning to the sound of a beautiful bird singing out my window. The warm beams of the sun filled a perfectly blue sky. *It was a great day for baseball.*

After pulling my arms and legs through my stretchy (sometimes scratchy) uniform, I ate a delicious, hot breakfast consisting of my dad's homemade pancakes with slices of sizzling bacon on the side. As much as I enjoyed the food, I couldn't wait to pedal my bike as fast as possible over to the Little League field. I felt entirely free without a worry in the world. Baseball and freedom – I loved that feeling.

I was a good ball player, the kind to always be relied upon whether I pitched or played in the outfield. By age 11, I made the Stamford, Connecticut Little League All-Star, which was made up of the best fourteen 11-12 year-olds in the league. It was an incredible accomplishment to make the team and I was floored by my good fortune.

Although we were knocked out at the District Finals level that year, I watched the Little League World Series Championship game on television a few weeks later. Back in 1982, the U.S. Little League team hadn't won the world championship game in about fifteen years, and a team from Washington ended up reclaiming the title with a 6-0 win. I thought it would be cool to play on that field at next year's game, and I imagined myself playing there.

Throughout the next year, I enjoyed my life by doing what it was I absolutely loved to do – play baseball, and then head over on my bike to the Reddy Rooster for fried chicken, spicy French fries and ice cream with my friends after practice.

Amazingly, one year later, we played in the Little League World Series US Championship game. The winner would go to the world final the very next day to play the Dominican Republic. The chances of us playing in this game had to be at least a million to one, though, because we lost our first game in the tournament. After that crushing blow, we had to win 19 straight games to make it to the U.S. final.

Here we were in the U.S. final – Stamford, Connecticut versus Marietta, Georgia. As the visiting team, we were up to bat first. We scored 5 runs in the top of the first inning, and Marietta scored 0 in the bottom half. I ran into the dugout high fiving my teammates, and yelled, "We're going to be on ABC Wide World of Sports tomorrow!"

Back then this was the only Little League World Series game to be televised nationally. However, my joy may have been a little preemptive. In the bottom of the 2nd inning, Marietta scored three runs. Our coach walked out to the mound, talked to the pitcher, and then pointed to me in left field – a moment of truth. It was time for me to take the reins and pitch. Electricity surged through my body; I wanted this.

After five innings, the game was tied 8-8. In the top of the sixth and last inning, we had the heart of the order up but remained scoreless. In the bottom of the sixth, Marietta had the bases loaded with two outs. The leadoff hitter stood at home plate, and I threw a fastball right down the middle. Crack! Line drive down the first base line. Our first baseman made a valiant effort, but the ball trailed off his mitt. Game over.

Then it happened. I heard this profound and loud Voice: "*I'm preparing you.*"

As Marietta celebrated and our team headed to the dugout, I looked around for the Voice. *Who said that?* My surprise can still be seen on the video recording. I'm sure that the onlookers chalked it up to the overwhelm of a young boy who had just lost the game.

When we left the stadium, I saw Keith Jackson with Earl Weaver, both of whom had announced the game. As Mr. Jackson signed my mitt, he looked me straight in the eyes and said, "Forte [he pronounced it "forty"], you have a lot of heart." I walked away, wondering, "*Is that where the Voice came from? My heart?*"

CHAPTER 2

That Big, Human False Belief: I'm Not Good Enough

As I grew up, I wondered about that Voice. What was it? What did it mean when it told me *"I am preparing you?"* But by the time I landed in high school, my attention had turned to other things, like baseball, girls and weightlifting. In general, school felt like a prison. Once in a while, I had a teacher or class that held my attention, but mostly, I was bored. Still, I managed to attain "good enough" grades, at least by my own estimation.

I was content with the B's and C's I received on my first high school report card, but my parents' disappointment lay heavy in the air. As I fidgeted in the backseat, I could see my dad's eyes in the rear-view mirror, glued to the road ahead. His body looked tense and I couldn't quite tell what was wrong or how to make it better, but the question he proposed to me seemed innocent enough. His eyes still focused on the road, he asked, "What are you going to do with your life, Chris?"

"Simple!" I enthusiastically answer with a grin on my face, "I'm going to be a professional baseball player." Although smiling, I was serious, because I'd put a lot of thought and energy into this decision.

"Chris, do you realize how hard it is to play in the Major Leagues? The chances are practically impossible. Do you know how big and fast you need to be? Do you realize there are only 700 Major League baseball players in the game?" On and on he babbled about the impossibility of my dream and how all of the odds were stacked against me.

"Motherfucking dream crusher…" I was 14 and I was *livid*. Even more potently, I felt devastated, shaken to my core. In one conversation, my dad had used "logic" to destroy my heart.

My dad is a good man. When I was a young boy, he spent hours playing catch with me in the front yard. He even struggled to bend down and play catcher when I pitched to him. But after my Little League days, that bond broke. In particular, it was this conversation at 14 that completely dismantled our relationship. *"Is this what a parent is supposed to do?"* I wondered.

After that incident with my dad, I became an angry young man. Unfortunately, I took my anger out on everyone, including my very lovely high school girlfriend. I often treated her with disrespect. I didn't know how to talk to people about my feelings or share about what was going on with me internally. I didn't have mentors or know who to reach out to. Most importantly, I didn't even know how to understand myself. Then something happened in the spring two weeks before freshman baseball tryouts…

I came down with mono. I couldn't believe it. I had been waiting all year for the tryout, and then wham, mono. I left school for two weeks and lost fifteen pounds. Looking back with what I now know about the body, I carried so much anger and hurt that my body had to give me a wake-up call. All of those repressed emotions and feelings had created a toxic sludge house that needed to be released somehow.

Although I was potentially contagious, one week of bedrest was about all I could take. I'd watched the older guys lifting weights in our school weight room, and even though 14 was a little young, I pleaded with my parents to buy me a bench and weights so I could work out at home. They honored my request, and thus began my love affair with weight lifting.

I had no idea how to train, but it felt so good. I loved it. I worked out alone and I worked hard. I ended up making the freshman baseball team, but something within me had shifted. I'd rather have been working out than doing anything else, and I loved working out alone. I felt free again, unencumbered by other peoples' judgments and expectations. Although I wouldn't have called it that then, in these moments, alone in my weight room, I felt close to God.

At 15, I built my basement sanctuary. I had a bench, dumbbells, a weight machine that attached to the wall, and my prized possession, my boxing Punching Bag. At this time in my life, my sanctuary was everything, then baseball, and then everything else.

I dealt with all my emotions by lifting weights in the basement. When I felt anger, I pounded that bag until my knuckles bled. I drove my parents crazy hitting that thing, as it shook the whole house with its reverberations. My mom had many little statues in our family room, and every morning after my workout, they would all be facing different directions on the shelves.

Once in awhile after an intense workout, completely exhausted and recovering, I would hear that Voice again: "I'm preparing you."

I ignored it most of the time, excusing it as my mind racing through a thought. What else could I do?

CHAPTER 3

The Voice Returns to Issue an Assignment

A short time later, my parents awkwardly announced that they had both lost their jobs. The losses had occurred within two weeks of one another. I felt like the rug had just been pulled out from under my family. My parents were good people, hard workers. I couldn't believe what I'd just heard. *What was going to happen to my brother and me?* Naturally, I headed downstairs to my sanctuary to hit the bag.

I punched and I punched and I hit and I punched. Then I hit the bag some more. I kept going until I couldn't feel my hands. My shoulders were on fire. I have no idea how long I stayed in the basement, but at some point I fell to the floor in a puddle of complete exhaustion. It was in that moment that the Voice came back.

"Always work for yourself. One day you will work for me. I'm preparing you."

Profound, deep, and crystal clear.

I calmly walked up to my younger brother's bedroom and repeated the directive to him: "Matt, always work for yourself, and you will be taken care of." That faith has carried me through many difficult times, and my faith IS my freedom today.

After my parents lost both of their jobs, life in our house started to slowly disintegrate and spiral downward. My Dad couldn't bounce back, and I lost respect for him daily as I watched my mom, this 5'1" pit bull, dig deep. Mom found a new job as an Office Manager and worked her ass off. My dad tried to do some things on his own, such as consulting work, but nothing he pursued seemed to work. So, the burden of paying the bills continuously fell onto my mom.

It wasn't long before my dad turned into a daily drinker. Unfortunately, alcohol consumption spiraled out of control for my mom as well. My dad ended up in Alcoholics Anonymous eventually, but for my mom, it would take the passage of time and a very serious wake-up call at night before things would change. It was at a time when I desperately needed a miracle – and I received one.

CHAPTER 4

Miracle on the Merritt

When the phone rang, the last person I expected to hear on the other end was my mother's co-worker. "Your mother's been drinking, and I don't think it's safe for her to drive."

My heart pounded. "I'll be right there!" I felt worried and protective, anxiously eager to pick up my mom and return her home from a dangerous situation. This was also a momentous responsibility to fall on the shoulders of a high school student.

When I arrived, I immediately noticed the glassiness in her eyes.

"Chris, I'm fine," she said, and pushed me away with some laughs. She told me to follow her car, and in that moment, I betrayed my own instincts. I jumped into my car and pulled out behind her. My gut wrenched and my muscles tightened.

I tapped the steering wheel with white knuckles, hunched forward. "It's only one mile, it's only one mile…" I told myself. Once we made it off the parkway, I decided I would drive in front of her, cut her off, and insist that she get in my car.

As we headed up the onramp, her car swerved back and forth. She weaved through the lanes of traffic, traveling over 70 mph, and cars raced around her, barely able to avoid being hit.

"NO! NO! NO!" I screamed. Tears rolled down my cheeks. I had no control over this terrifying sight. It felt like time slowed down. I was sure I was about to watch my mom crash her car and kill herself or someone else. Out of sheer desperation and panic, I yelled, "Jesus, help! Jesus, help! Jesus, help!"

Then I witnessed a miracle. I could hardly believe what I was seeing, even as it played out right in front of me. We had just sped down the parkway for a mile already. We had swerved in and out of all the lanes as I'd tried to keep up with her. The car suddenly started coasting smoothly at 15-20 mph. She cruised slowly off the exit ramp, pulled over and parked. Her eyes were still glassy, and she still claimed she was fine to drive.

I was in shock. I exited my car like a robot, hopped into my mom's car, and drove her home. Not only was my body and mind shaken from the experience of this near tragedy, but I couldn't wrap my mind around what seemed like the Divine intervention I had just called in and witnessed.

My father, brother, aunt, uncle and co-worker joined me in staging an intervention for my mom after that dreadful night. As I sat listening to all of the stories about why they wanted my mom to recover, all I wanted to do was leave. I had already been avoiding home and my parents for some time. I'd even spent Thanksgiving with friends. I was about to bolt out of the room when I heard the Voice say, "Let's help your Mom." So, I stayed.

When it came my time to share my truth about my mother with everyone, I cried like I've never cried before. Water poured out of my eyes that I didn't even know existed in my body. I struggled to express the words caught in my throat… "Mom, I love you… Mom, you need help…"

Obviously shaken, she came over to me, sat on my lap, kissed me on the head, and said, "Okay." She made the decision to recover. It was the hardest she had ever seen me cry. Relief flooded my body.

My uncle drove my mom to a Betty Ford clinic. As I watched her walk out of the house, I instinctively knew that my parent's marriage was over. All the tension over the years had come to a head due to my father's work and financial instability and my mother's drinking. Therefore, it came as no surprise when I received a phone call from my mother saying they were divorcing.

My mom remained sober throughout my years in college, and I began to focus on my own life, which meant pursuing my dreams to become a professional baseball player.

CHAPTER 5

Chasing, Chasing, Chasing Freedom

I did it. I walked on the field and made the Division 1 baseball team at the University of Dayton. The baseball tryouts occurred right when I arrived on campus. It was early September. We trained every day until the Thanksgiving break. The day after New Year's, the daily training resumed. College baseball training involved much more of my time than my high school baseball training. In fact, it took up more of my time than anything I'd ever attempted to do to date. I felt constrained, which left me in a peculiar dilemma. This was exactly what I had wanted to do for years, but I started to question my choice. *"Do I love this anymore?* A big part of me wanted to join my friends, have fun and party – you know, engage in the college experience.

I stayed with the training for baseball for the year and focused on my school work as well. My GPA was the best it had ever been in all of my schooling because of that structure, but something was missing. Freedom. Baseball no longer felt like fun and play.

Because of my training and my reputation for playing at 100%, I became a starter in left field for our first game at Ohio State. It was early March. The temperature was freezing and snow covered the grass. Some of my buddies made the ride from Dayton to cheer me on. I saw their case of beer, and in that moment, my baseball career was over. I realized I wanted to be with my friends, rather than be on the field.

Letting go of baseball felt a bit like letting go of the dreams of the child I once was. It felt like a rite of passage into adulthood. Dad was right – being a professional ball player would be tough. The truth was, I didn't want it, nor was I willing to do the necessary work to become a professional ballplayer.

After a few games I lost my starting position, but finished the season.

During the last game I told one of the seniors on the team that I would not be coming back. That's when he posed a life-changing question to me: "Forte, have you ever bet on baseball?"

The idea of betting on baseball games intrigued me. This was a new game I could play, and besides, it appeared to be a great way to make money. This senior showed me the ropes. We placed bets every day for two weeks before I headed home with $500 in my pocket. I was hooked. I didn't yet realize that in my yearning for freedom, I would first become enslaved.

When I returned home, my friend, Eric, and I planned to land in Hilton Head for the summer. Eric and I had been friends since second grade. Hundreds of times we'd played two-hand touch football, street hockey and wiffle ball in his cul-de-sac. Now, as young men, our plan was to find work and an apartment, and do what college kids do at Hilton Head in the summer – hang out at the beach, party at night, work hung over, and repeat the next day.

When we arrived, we found it difficult to find jobs or a place to live. All the cheap rentals were taken by other college kids, because we started late. So, we booked a hotel room for a couple of nights to figure out what to do.

Before we left for Hilton Head, I had been introduced to a bookie. Since we couldn't find work, I said to Eric, "How about we bet on some baseball games? If we win, we can use that money for rent on a nice condo. If we lose, we head home." Well, we bet all week and won almost every game.

Something else happened to me. The rush was exhilarating, and it was an escape from reality. We won more than lost, and the bookie kept wiring us money. Within a couple of weeks, we'd raised enough money for our rent, food, and drink. Life was good.

Through good times and bad times, I would continue betting for the next four-and-a-half-years. I became a social drinker and even an occasional drug user, but gambling… gambling was my thing. Ultimately, I would learn that I could hide my gambling from the outside world, but I could not hide it from myself.

CHAPTER 6

Escape to Rock Bottom, then Lifted Up into a Deeper Truth

I sought that sense of solitary freedom I'd loved as a child, but the way I went about it got twisted. Sure, I still took care of my body – at least in theory – but gambling became my sanctuary. Through gambling I felt like myself – uninhibited, but more "free" of feelings than "free to be me." For example, I felt free of other peoples' judgments and rules, and free of the pain of the feelings I didn't know how to handle. In my wildest dreams, I never thought I'd trade my childhood dreams of a career in professional baseball for a career in professional sports betting, but I treated it like a business, and one that was more realistic, at that.

I managed to make it through many highs and lows. In a way, gambling helped me through college and through the pain of my parents' divorce. I needed an escape from my feelings then, because I didn't have other tools to cope with the changes in my life. I had never been taught how to express my emotions, and I grasped at straws to understand what it meant to evolve into manhood. But the more I sunk into the escape that gambling provided for me, the more I became devoid of real happiness beyond the big wins. Nevertheless, I graduated with a degree in marketing.

Fresh out of college, I moved to Chicago where I quickly scored a job as a sales executive for a telecom company. It was a perfect complement to my gambling life. I hit the phones and worked hard for the telecom company to make sure I was at, or above, quota in the first two weeks of every month. This strategy allowed me to keep focused on my gambling, so I could maintain that false sense of freedom I derived from it. As the years passed, I became more and more preoccupied with the high of winning.

However, like any addiction, there came a point when gambling stopped giving me that high. I functioned like a stressed out zombie pursuing a mirage that beckoned me down hollow roads that collapsed when I approached. One day, I could no longer recognize the man who looked back at me in the mirror.

Where is my freedom? What happened to me? Not only was my body slipping, but I lived in a state of constant anxiety. I felt completely lost. I owed money to bookies and many other people. I was so filled with stress and disillusionment that I couldn't get myself out of bed in the morning.

It wasn't like the suicidal thoughts that followed slid in out of nowhere. The despair, the hopelessness, the feelings of disillusionment and loss—these feelings first showed up when I pitched that losing hit in the Little League World Series. They had been a familiar companion ever since, sometimes like a shadow that disappeared when I looked at it, and other times appearing to be more prominent. The weightlifting, the money, the wins—I LOVED those high highs. I adored feeling on top of the world. By gambling, I was just doing what felt right. But I couldn't escape the feeling that something was missing.

One frigid December night, I realized I had hit rock bottom. Having tapped out all of my friends, family, and even acquaintances, I had no one left to borrow money from, not even a dime. My self-respect had disintegrated like my fading memories of summertime baseball. $500 stared back at me in my checking account. But I needed to come up with $12,000 by the next morning.

Any sense of freedom I might have felt disappeared as I paced my house in my boxers, sweating, trembling, and sick. I had no idea how to come up with this large sum of money. At that moment, it seemed like it would be easier for me to kill myself and end my pain.

Freedom to me had meant a life without worry, anxiety and stress. It represented a life filled with love, joy and peace. I had been chasing this ideal of freedom for years, and clearly, I had come up short.

I was done – with everything. I made a decision to end my life, and that decision gave me a sense of peace.

I calmly strode into the bathroom and turned the water on to fill the tub. Then I took another step towards my end, and fell onto my hands and knees. I sobbed on the floor, naked, prepared to die. I guess a part of me did die that night, the part that no longer supported me in my life. Perhaps I had to allow that part of me to die in order for something greater to be born.

"Boy, I love you. Get up, call home."

A warm feeling enveloped me, like a calming and completely serene blanket had just been wrapped around me. I felt like a newborn baby. I couldn't stop crying even as a gentle force pulled me to my feet, compassionately removing the effort it would have taken me to stumble to my feet on my own. But I wasn't alone now. Time had come to a standstill for the second time in my life. All I felt was light, enveloping peace, and a sense of gentle sunlight and warmth. I have never felt as loved as in that moment.

As I looked into the mirror with tears rolling down my face, I suddenly recognized the Voice. I'd always wondered if that voice was actually the voice of one of the baseball announcers, or if it had come from my imagination or from my own inner voice—but staring back at that face I barely recognized in the mirror, and feeling that deep sense of peace that enveloped me, I realized that, all along, the Voice had been the Voice of God.

I was in the care of God. It had been God, who had talked to me on the baseball mound. It was God who told me He was preparing me. And I realized it was God who talked to me in the basement as I pounded that punching bag all of those years.

I also immediately recognized that it really had been Jesus who had been the one who saved my mom on the parkway. This feeling of being lifted to my feet was surely the same benevolent force that had taken control of her swerving car and coasted it to safety.

It was all God. God had been with me always. Even in my bleakest, most disconnected moment, it was still God. It was always God. I also knew powerfully in my heart that *God would never leave me, and that I never had to feel alone again.*

I splashed some water on my face and looked into my eyes with a sense of resolution and renewed purpose. Only ten minutes earlier I had been taking steps to end my life, but now, now I obeyed the Voice. Slowly, and with a new sense of truth, love, and deep knowing, I picked up my phone and called my parents.

Because of their experience with Alcoholics Anonymous, they recommended I go to Gamblers Anonymous. So, I located a meeting and attended it that night. The moment I took this first step to get healthy the feeling of hopelessness and despair vanished. Somehow, I knew that things were going to be different, even though I still had to deal with the $12,000 debt I'd incurred.

My dad flew out to Chicago to spend Christmas with me. I was in awe of the fact that my dad was now celebrating the holiday with me in the very same house where I had been completely ready to end my life just a few weeks prior.

I attended more Gamblers Anonymous meetings, but even though I could see it working for some people, it wasn't the right place for me. That being said, the guys at Gamblers Anonymous shared their wisdom and experiences with me to help me straighten things out with my bookie. They helped me come up with a payment plan, and for two straight years, I made a payment of $500 cash per month to pay back the bookie. I'll always remember that final payment when I handed the bookie five 100-dollar bills.

As I limped along in my recovery, I knew I needed to make my relationship with God number one in my life and to somehow keep moving forever, even though I had no idea what my path would look like. I decided it would be a good way to start by taking better care of my body, so I joined a gym and began lifting weights.

Every time, a problem arose, I turned it over to my Higher Power the best I could and humbly tried to learn what my addictive behavior was teaching me. By gambling, I had chased freedom right into the depths of hell. My false sense of reality had become my best friend. I thought about all the times I rode my bike to the Little League Field. Those were moments of connecting with God in true joy and true freedom. When I built my weight room, my sanctuary, I felt like I was also in the presence of God. In contrast, gambling had been an entirely selfish act in which I'd become disconnected from everyone – and especially from God. But God had never given up on me.

When I couldn't figure out the answers to some of my bigger questions, I felt frustrated. *Why did I do this to myself? Why did I put myself in this situation? What was the lesson I needed to learn?*

Although I was comforted by knowing that God was with me, I struggled to make meaning of the past decade, so I kept digging deeper. I needed to return to some of the healthy places where I'd heard the Voice and felt that profound sense of peace and freedom before gambling took over my life. I needed a chance to discover some of these answers, and I felt that they would come in time if I maintained an open heart and mind, my curiosity, and my yearning for freedom.

And that is why I went back to my weight room, my sanctuary. I needed to look inside myself and slow down. I needed to listen to the messages Spirit had for me. Once I was working out in my weight room sanctuary, I felt like I was back on track. I added running and swimming to the mix. This time around, I felt the Presence of God in my life; God was my partner in weight lifting, my "spiritual spotter".

Knowing that He was with me dramatically changed my awareness. I started a telecom business with two partners shortly thereafter. I also was lucky enough to fall in love with a special woman who would become my wife one year later. Things were definitely on the up and up.

CHAPTER 7

Living the "American Dream"

By age 29, it appeared that I had all the trappings of success. I was happily married, had a 6-month-old daughter, and my telecom business was booming. After making a visit to a priest when my wife was a few months pregnant, I'd performed my first confession in over a decade. Ever since that time, I had been maintaining a daily discipline of doing the rosary prayer practice, and it had become a huge part of my life. My intention was to build and foster a stronger connection with God. So, every morning, I sat with my coffee, counted the prayers bead by bead, and recited a specific prayer.

At this time, the money was rolling in, and my company was constantly being pursued by acquires, which would make me a multimillionaire overnight. As far as what I believed a "healthy, happy man's life" should look like, all of the boxes were checked:

✓ *Beautiful wife? Check.*
✓ *Successful, self-led business and self-made man? Check.*
✓ *Child? Check.*

✓ *Strong body? Yep, check.*
✓ *Money in the bank and material success? Check.*

As I continued to build my relationship with God daily through my rosary practice, and even with all of these pieces in place, something still didn't feel quite right; something was missing. I felt empty, but I couldn't figure out why. *What was wrong with me? I had accomplished everything I was supposed to work for in life by now. Why wasn't I happy?*

My unhappiness led my wife and I to couples therapy, and after a few sessions, I started seeing a therapist on my own. After my first session with the new therapist, she handed me a book called "The Alchemist." I immediately drove home and read it from cover to cover. Each page touched my spirit and soul. I resonated with the main character's search to find a hidden treasure, only to realize that the treasure was to find himself. For the first time in my life, I felt passionate about learning more about spirituality and my personal journey.

At the age of 31, I started writing in my journal, prompted by an intuitive desire to learn to express myself and feel better in a new way. Just like hitting the bag at the gym let off anger, I found that writing released emotions, too. I didn't seek it out. I just found myself picking up a notebook at work one day, and I started writing to God. After that first notebook, I started writing more deeply in my journals. Writing was something I realized I could count on to help me work through different issues in my life.

In those journals, I wrote about everything – the ups and downs in my business, my relationship with my wife, being a father, and being a man. Journal writing also gave me another way to pray and communicate with God. The rosary, writing, journaling, reading, and exercise were now part of my daily routine, and back then I had no idea I had created a certain lifestyle that would consistently lead me in a positive and uplifting direction.

CHAPTER 8

Listening to the Universe's Nudges

Although I was taking better care of myself every day, I was surprised to discover through my writing, therapy, and workouts that the telecom business I had created and co-founded no longer inspired me. It was a career I didn't want to do anymore. It felt like yet another prison, since the duties and responsibilities of my specific role had changed over the years, which didn't bring me the fulfillment I thought it would. No passion. No fun. The money was excellent. I didn't see a way out, even though I was bored, restless, and ready for something new.

In the midst of my uneasiness, something strange seemingly happened out of "nowhere." Rosland, a trainer in my company, handed me a book she was excited about called, *Rich Dad, Poor Dad*. I immediately plopped it down on my credenza where it sat for weeks.

One day my curiosity – or boredom, or intuition – urged me to open the book. Just like *The Alchemist* before, I consumed the knowledge within it. Within a week, this little book about real estate prompted my wife and I to sell our townhouse and move to our summer house on Lake Michigan. The smell of fresh air, water, and beach was heaven. It was the perfect place for me to relax, unwind, and just enjoy life.

Once we settled in, we continued to follow the wisdom in the book and created a plan to buy rental properties. Our idea was that as soon as the cash flow was coming in to support us, I would leave my company in Chicago.

However the move to the lake meant a 90-minute commute to Chicago almost daily. To help ease the commute, I stayed with my sister and brother in-law, part of the week and worked from home on Fridays. Meanwhile, on the home front, my wife handled the properties we bought and also took care of our two girls. Within a short time, a third daughter was born.

With three young girls to raise, as well as the work we needed to do to build our residential real estate portfolio, it made sense to us to invite my dad to live with us. My father proved to be very valuable in helping us. He showed all the properties while my wife filled out all the applications, credit checks, etc. I bought the properties, financed the loans from the bank, and met the tenants. Our three-person system worked well together.

One Monday morning, as I headed to Chicago in my dad's car, I noticed a cross hanging from the rearview mirror. My eyes riveted on it.

"Ask for it," the Voice commanded. So, I asked for it, and my dad gave it to me. The moment I placed the cross on my rearview mirror the nature of my commute changed.

During the 90-minute commute, I started pretending that Jesus was a passenger sitting next to me in the front seat. I talked to him like he was a friend – a regular guy. We talked about everything in my life – the obstacles I encountered in my company and especially about being a husband and a father. I started to realize I could tap into God all the time.

After 18 months, my commute came to an end, as I was in a strong enough position to leave the day-to-day running of my company. I'd only have to go to Chicago for the occasional board meeting. My dilemma was that I would no longer have that special time with Jesus. So, I started doing the rosary while taking walks in the woods, went for runs, which became a new form of meditation, and swam and kayaked in the lake. Through these activities, I integrated the knowledge that Christ was a being whose energy could be tapped into at any time by anyone who desired that connection.

In addition to my ongoing physical activities, I also prioritized reading and writing. To a large degree, I felt content, but always a seeker, I yearned for an even deeper connection with God. It was only in those moments when I felt a connection to God that I felt free and aligned with my true being.

Living my life fulltime on the lake, I was curious about how my connection with God might grow, but I had no idea as to the extent that my spirituality was about to blossom and deepen.

One day, my muscles felt tense. So, I looked for a local place where I could receive a holistic massage. I came across a little place downtown that simply said, "Massage" with an accompanying phone number. The storefront looked reputable, so I called the number and left a message.

A few days later, my cell phone rang.

The caller said, "Hello, I'm Linda. I don't usually return calls, but for some reason I felt I should call you back regarding your massage."

That seemed like an odd response, given that she had advertised her phone number along with the word, "Massage," right on her door, but I let the thought go.

"Thank you for the call back. I've been getting massages regularly in Chicago, and I'm looking for someone local," I explained.

"I don't do massages," she responded. "I do energy work and I'm a body worker. I do need to change that sign."

Intrigued, I scheduled an appointment. I had never heard of "energy work," and I was curious to experience it.

A couple of weeks later, I lay on her table, totally unprepared for this amazing energetic experience that was about to unfold. She didn't touch my skin, yet I could feel a tingling electrical sensation all throughout my body. After the session, I felt so recharged I could have run a marathon.

"What was that, Linda?"

She replied, "Energy work. I don't work on many adults. I usually work with children."

Shortly thereafter, Linda invited my wife and I to her office. She showed us how she did energy work on her granddaughter. We were amazed to see this little girl. Before the session, she was like a little wiggle worm. She climbed all over the place. But by the time Linda finished, this child displayed such a sense of peace it took my breath away. We observed her as she lay on her side all curled up like a little baby. Her eyes were closed. She breathed deeply and her ribs slowly expanded. She exuded such a state of tranquility.

We decided to invite Linda to our house so we could learn more about her and decide if we wanted to have her work with our children. Until this point, my spiritual practices included my rosary, developing my relationships with God and with Jesus, writing, reading, and getting daily exercise. I hadn't been exposed to any holistic healing practices. My heart whispered to me, "This woman can teach you things you need to know."

Still, I wasn't quite sure about whether I could trust what she offered, as energy work was completely foreign to my world view and experience, so I posed a question. "Are you religious, Linda?"

"No," she said, "but I work with the Christ Energy."

I had no idea what that meant, but a directive came forth from the Voice: *"Work with this woman."*

From that day onwards, Linda continued to perform energy work on myself and the children. She became both my mentor and dear friend, and over the next twelve years, I learned everything I could from her regarding energy work, bodywork, essential oils, healing, chakras, breathing, eating, and – most importantly – children.

I learned that all humans have male and female energies, and I learned about the ratio of male and female energies within my own body. Since my male side was dominant, in order for me to achieve a better balance of male and female energies, she encouraged me to shift from the "male provider" role, and cultivate more qualities associated with female energy, such as nurturance, playfulness, and affection.

I took Linda's advice to heart, and I began with my children. Instead of just dropping my girls off at school and picking them up and taking them to classes, I spent my afternoons sitting on the living room floor with them playing Barbies and having Barbie parties. Every week, we put on a play. Our most famous show was called, "Pierre and Franco", which featured two French gay hairstylists who owned a hair salon in Paris.

Linda taught me that my body was made up of energy, and that my unexpressed emotions were stored in my body, only to surface as pain later on. From my gentle entry into the realm of holistic healing through Linda's work, my curiosity continued to grow. I explored a smorgasbord of energy-based approaches, from Shamanic healers, to acupuncturists, mystical professionals who did past-life regressions, to numerologists, astrologers and clairvoyants.

I was a sponge. I sopped up every bit of knowledge I could. It became evident in my explorations that I needed to heal the emotional wounds I'd incurred from my childhood – especially concerning the wound around my relationship with my father. He had squashed my childhood dream, and I had witnessed his plunge into the abyss of alcohol abuse. Many emotions needed to surface in order for me to heal.

Our realities of the way we lived in the world were completely different.

Ultimately, I realized that my father had always done what he thought was best for me with the qualities he possessed at that specific moment in time.

I also learned to acknowledge and accept that I was raised by two individuals with whom I didn't have a strong positive connection. But the biggest epiphany came when I realized I had the ability to change the fractured relationships I had with each of them: *I needed to end the blame game and forgive them for not having lived up to my standards.*

The clearer my awareness became, the more I realized that my wife and I had a spiritual disconnect. She wasn't as taken by Linda's energy work as I was. We used to walk together around our beautiful property, but we never enjoyed the outdoors together anymore. We had stopped sharing our thoughts and feelings, and we no longer asked each other what we needed from the other. The intimate bond we'd once shared was missing, and our relationship felt pretty superficial. We still cared for each other, as one might when they've known someone for a long time, but we were drifting apart. I wanted us to come back together. Perhaps a change of scenery would help.

CHAPTER 9

Changes in Space, Changes in Relationship

On St. Patty's Day, we moved from the lake to a town near Detroit called, Birmingham. It had been very challenging to raise three little girls while we lived at the lake house. Driving to the store always felt like a field trip, and the school was located ten miles away. I prayed that our new life in Birmingham would make things easier, and that this change would be good for us.

As my goodbye to Lake Michigan, I took a pair of rosary beads, put it in my kayak, and pushed the vessel out into the lake. I released the kayak and rosary beads as a gratitude to God, and as a way to showcase my faith in the Divine's will for my life, as well as my gratitude for all that I had been given up until that point. I felt that whoever found that kayak was meant to receive it as a gift.

Life in the new house wasn't as smooth as I'd hoped it would be. We chugged away at our real estate business, but it remained a struggle. The financial crisis of 2008 was about to hit. Fortunately, my telecom company in Chicago sold in the nick of time. The buyer even wanted to fast track the money to me, which was a blessing. However, when he sent the wire for 5½ million dollars to my account at Citibank, the bank was on the verge of going under.

Frantically, I called my banker and ordered an immediate transfer of the funds to my local bank. What should have been a time of celebration turned out to be a full day of nonstop stress. Thank goodness the money came through, because when the market crashed, our real estate business went entirely down the tubes.

I was grateful I had three important things in place: my family, my commitment to God, and my daily spiritual practice. I reflected back on the times that the Voice had been there with me before, and even though I couldn't hear those words now, I knew in my heart that I still was not alone.

But it had been twelve years since I last heard the Voice, when it had guided me to work with Linda. *Why hadn't I heard the Voice in all these years? Was I doing something wrong?* I communicated daily with God, hoping for an answer.

CHAPTER 10

"Be Your Truth and Trust All is in Divine Order"

For my 39th birthday, I wanted to do something special to commemorate my connection with God, the Universe, my mentor/friend Jesus, and the spiritual aspects of my life. I gave myself the present of a beautiful tattoo – of a crucifix, which covered my left shoulder. The word, "Truth", was spelled out vertically inside the cross, and the word, "Trust", ran horizontally. The "U" in both words intersected in the middle. The cross would always remind me of my friendship with Jesus and prompt me to remember how my mentor had lived, and that he had died for doing what he loved – spreading the message of God. The ultimate sacrifice.

My wife and the girls joined me at the tattoo parlor. While the girls seemed excited and intrigued, my wife said, "I would never get a tattoo". I respected her path, but I felt hurt because she didn't know how important this new image on my arm was to me. Inking the cross on my body meant a lot more to me than just decorating my skin with a random tattoo. This tattoo represented my commitment.

Also on that day, I further committed to treat my body as a gift from God. I made the commitment to take the steps to live a healthier life in body, mind, and spirit. After having smoked socially for 20 years, I quit cold turkey. I became conscious of the types of food and liquids I put in my body, and added High Intensity Training, boxing, and CrossFit to my daily exercise regimen.

But after the thrill of the tattoo wore off, I engaged in the motions of life without truly being present – even in my daily spiritual practices and concerning my relationship with God. The "sleepwalking years" ticked on, and struggle seemed to surround me on every side. The limping real estate business had reduced its value by 50%, meaning the money I relied on to support my family disappeared. Two other businesses I'd started also simultaneously fell apart.

I sat and drank wine alone at night, and watched mindless TV shows after I tucked the girls into bed. My wife and I lived separate lives. Even when the dog needed to be walked, we walked him individually, instead of hand in hand like we used to. She went to a lot of social events that I had no interest in. For all intents and purposes, we weren't partners anymore, we were roommates.

One spring day while I was out jogging, something suddenly hit me. My intuition told me something was off with my wife. I gently confronted her when I got home.

"I'm showing my vulnerability here. Are you in contact with anyone?"

"No, Chris. No," she calmly replied.

"Facebook, anything? Something isn't right."

"No, Chris." She remained steadfast in her response.

My head and logical mind told me, "believe her", but my heart jumped to red alert. *Where was the Voice? Why hadn't I heard it in years?* I had been praying for clarity and direction as to what to do with my business and in regards to my relationship with my wife. Still, I did not receive any answers.

However, one day while out jogging, I suddenly heard the lilting song of a bird nearby. It was the same beautiful sound that had awakened me to go play baseball on a bright, sunny day as a boy. I hadn't heard this bird's song for over thirty years, and I recognized the significance of it immediately; it was a sign. I realized the Universe, through the sound of this little bird, was trying to catch my attention. I had been feeling so confused, lost, hopeless, and abandoned that I dropped to my hands and knees and started sobbing. I didn't know what to do next, but for the first time in a very long time, I felt a glimmer of hope. *How could I find out more about this bird? What was its message for me?*

CHAPTER 11

It Takes Two to Marry and Two to Divorce

My answer would come in a most unexpected way...

In February 2014, I attended a men's retreat. Although I really wanted to open up and share with the group about the serious breakdown in my relationship with my wife, I held back. I didn't want to violate the privacy I still felt obliged to honor in my relationship with my wife.

Then, on the last day of the retreat, I participated in an archery activity, and in the midst of shooting arrows, there it was again – the sound of that bird, ringing loud and clear. What were the odds that the man standing next to me would be an avid bird watcher?

"Frank, that's the bird!" I'd told the men a little bit about the bird before.

Frank wasn't sure about its identity, but he whistled to it, and the bird responded. Frank recorded the sound on his iPhone as they "sang" back and forth to one another. Twenty-four hours later, I received a text message: "Chris, it's a Black-Capped Chickadee."

I grabbed my *Animal Speak* book by Ted Andrews to learn about the bird. I knew this bird was my spirit animal. According to Andrews, the Black-Capped Chickadee was "the Bird of Truth". One of the main characteristics of the chickadee was that, upon hearing its beautiful song, individuals were enabled to express their truth with others more joyfully. And by expressing that truth, they were able to share their innermost feelings with one another in a loving manner – even if that truth hurt. When I read the description of the Black-Capped Chickadee, I knew that the time was getting closer for me to express more of my truth, even though I knew that my truth would lead me straight into a storm with my spouse.

Four months later, we had dinner and drinks with some friends. Afterwards, I wanted to go home, but she wanted to stay out. All the husbands were tired, including me, so I drove home while all the wives stayed out for more drinks. When I returned home, I sat out on the porch thinking about how sad it was that our marriage had slipped away, and that the life we had created was not working. I picked her up some hours later, thinking my marriage was crumbling. When we went to bed that night, I couldn't fall asleep. I paced around our bedroom asking God for help, but received no response.

As an effort to resolve our disconnect, we set an appointment with a holistic marriage counselor to sort things out. During the appointment and subsequent appointments, we parsed through our entire 17 year marriage and past history together. What I realized was that the spiritual disconnect between us had vastly widened since we'd moved to Birmingham in 2006. Both of us felt a sense of betrayal by the other for different reasons, and we could no longer find common ground outside of our children.

I needed some space, so I told my wife, "I'm leaving for the weekend. I'm heading to the lake. I need to be alone." I stayed at The Chalets on Lake Michigan, right next to my former house. Even though it felt like my world had crumbled, I knew it was important to keep showing up for myself the best I could, as this would keep me spiritually fit and able to better work through anything that came my way.

Even though I was burning with anger at God, I ran, walked on the beach, read, wrote, prayed, and meditated. Then, during one of my runs, I stopped in the middle of the road and screamed. Actually, I didn't just scream; I shattered the sound barrier. It was the biggest scream of my life, from the core of my being. I let the beast out, just as I had when I'd hit the punching bag in my parent's basement. I felt lied to, betrayed, disrespected, and a bit lost; I was a very hurt man.

I came home with renewed strength, hoping to continue to work through our issues with the holistic marriage counselor. I decided I would man up and follow in Jesus', my mentor's, footsteps (the best I could). I would enjoy the time I spent with my kids and make the best of the situation. Jesus had been my mentor since my mid-twenties because I had never found a male mentor in my life. Also, every time I encounter a problem, I would ask, "What would Jesus do?"

A few weeks later, we piled in the car and traveled to my wife's parent's house for the July 4th weekend. Shortly after arriving at their home, I decided to go for a run. About ¼ mile into the woods, I dropped to my knees. The Voice was speaking to me: "Chris, this will be the last time you run here."

In that moment, I made a choice. I decided to completely shift my attitude; I welcomed joy and peace into my life, regardless of the pain that this marriage had brought me to. The next three days were filled with fun and connection, which included my time with my wife. The girls and I jumped on the trampoline in the pond and played tag. Her father and I displayed fireworks at night, and later, my wife, the girls and I collected branches for a nighttime hotdog roast. We also walked around the property with the dogs that evening. I interacted with everyone and focused on what I was thankful for; I was grateful to be spending quality time with my family and to acknowledge her parents' presence in my life.

I realized I had the power within me to choose how to respond in this situation. It was futile for me to try to control my spouse or anyone else; all I could control was my response in any given situation.

As soon as we returned home, we visited the holistic marriage counselor. During the session, the counselor presented three options. The first option was to do nothing and continue the path we treaded on and pretend everything was okay. The second option was to get a divorce, and the third was to be in the present, move past the feelings of betrayal, dig deep, and do the work to maintain our marriage.

I said to my wife, "If we are to have a chance, we're going to have to fight through this together. If we can come out the other side, we will have the opportunity for a great marriage."

She replied, "Chris I don't want to fight."

Enveloped in sadness, I knew the marriage was over. Upon this disclosure, I badly needed my four-and-half mile run, and headed off to be with my thoughts. At the end of the sprint, my eyes closed and I calmly said: "God, I pray that this doesn't happen to another man. God, I'll do whatever you need to help me in this mission."

When I walked in the door I realized that I desperately needed to talk to someone. I had to grieve the end of my 17-year marriage and start to accept the reality that our divorce would be imminent. But I wasn't used to talking about my feelings; I had kept all of this information to myself for months without reaching out to loved ones for support. So, the first person I called was my sister.

"Can you meet me at the park? It's an emergency."

I struggled across the green as I saw my sister in the distance. She ran and caught me before I fell to the ground. I hugged her and let out the largest moan and cry of my life—even bigger than the one in Chicago from the time I'd curled up on the floor. Somehow, I felt even more vulnerable, and this was even more painful than the time I had faced my own desire to die. This felt like a different kind of death.

After I gained my composure, my sister asked, "Chris, are you dying?"

Her question made me laugh, which gave me a small sense of relief. I sat Indian-style on the picnic table, and she sat on the bench as I relayed the story of the last few months. She listened closely as I shared everything that was going on in my life. At the end of our conversation, which lasted more than an hour, she gave me a big hug and offered her support by reiterating that she was here for me in any capacity.

Over the next few months, my body had been reacting as well. My foot killed me, and I couldn't run. The pain in my heel was excruciating, and it even brought me to my knees at times. The doctor diagnosed the pain in my foot as planter's fasciitis. In addition, my emotions were all over the place, and I knew there existed a connection between my foot and the ending of my marriage. The pain in my foot represented that I needed to change. The running in my life, which ignited the pain in my foot, was not allowing me to adequately deal with the inner turmoil I was experiencing emotionally.

I tried boxing, High Intensity Training and CrossFit because I couldn't run. None of these physical fitness activities helped me with my emotional pain. No matter how many push-ups I did, I felt restless and unfulfilled.

Still, I had known this day would come when I would want to explore yoga again. I tried yoga six years prior, and although the physical part of the program did not resonate with me, the spiritual side and teachings intrigued me. I was initially attracted to the fact that yoga has both physical and spiritual benefits, and I thought the practice would help me work through my emotional pain at this time. Because none of the other activities were working and I was having difficulty dealing with my emotions, I decided to give yoga another try.

The end of a marriage is no easy thing. I tried to take care of myself the best I could. So, I attended yoga class in the morning and evening. I continued my rosary, read, wrote in my journal, and prayed big time for guidance. I also reached out to Linda.

Hearing me bawl on the phone, Linda gently said, "Chris, this has nothing to do with you. At the same time, you also need to take responsibility."

She was right. I had to take responsibility for my part in the marriage. It takes two to marry and it takes two to divorce. My entrepreneurial spirit had received major blows over the last eight years with three unsuccessful start-up companies. I didn't feel good about myself. I had isolated myself. I didn't share my feelings, stresses or concerns. I hadn't asked for my wife's help. Instead, I'd promised her a life of security and stability that had slowly chipped away over the years.

In my heart, and because of my past experiences in life, faith, and my trust in God, as well as my will to never give up, I knew this could all turn around for us. However, I hadn't listened to her and respected her feelings, like a true partner should.

When I dug deeper, I realized the divorce had nothing to do with my wife and had everything to do with my relationship with God, and my need to prioritize that relationship. The isolation I felt from God was me not listening to Him and that had spilled over into our marriage. Like when I hit rock bottom gambling, God came into my life again. This time God wanted to catch my attention. In truth, I wasn't angry at my wife; I was angry at myself for creating a life that wasn't working for me. What next?

One November morning as I practiced the Rosary, I stopped in the middle of it. Once in awhile that happened if I fell into prayer or a meditative state. This time, though, my heart told me to grab a pen and my journal. I opened my journal and as the pen hit the paper, these words effortlessly came out:

For My Highest Good, Let Her Go
For Her Highest Good, Let Her Go

For The Highest Good, Let Her Go
I Love Her, So Let Her Go
I Love Me, So Let Her Go

I called my wife and calmly said, "I'm filing for divorce." She cried on the other end of the line, as we both knew it was over for good. That same day, I met with my partners and called my investors and told them I was leaving the start-up company for personal reasons. In truth, I knew the days of leading this company were over, and I needed to focus on my physical, mental, emotional and spiritual well-being.

It was a very emotional night. My wife and I gathered the girls in Ava's room and told them that we loved each other but we didn't want to be married anymore. We all shed tears and hugged each other. Our dog Buddy helped, as our daughter, Simone, cuddled him on the floor.

I felt very grateful for the time I'd had with my wife. It was all purposeful. I prayed and sent a blessing of gratitude out into the Universe and released it: "*Lara, thank you for being a part of my life. Many blessings on your journey. Be Well.*"

Now I was ready to let go of my marriage, but the healing journey was far from over...

CHAPTER 12

Time to Dig Deep

I knew the healing process from the death of this marriage would take time. In addition, what would make the divorce and healing more challenging is that I wanted to change everything about my life – from the type of work I was doing, to the kinds of relationships I wanted to engage in, to the person inside of me that I wanted to bring out into the world. Where was I to start?

First, I moved into an apartment that was nearby my former wife's house. Then, I made a commitment to myself that for my well-being I would only do practices that could carry me through this difficult time. Truthfully, I wanted to leave for a year and go to a monastery, ashram, or a temple, but that wasn't in the cards. I had to be present for my three daughters, which meant that I had to perform this inner work while living my everyday life. In order to accomplish this, I made a commitment for six months to abstain from electronics, except for my cell phone, which would only be used for my daughters, holistic healers, Linda, and my family.

My daily regimen consisted of morning prayer, affirmations, rosary, and yoga, followed by a healthy breakfast of a banana spinach smoothie. I would meditate, write and read, and eat healthy snacks, like a green apple, almonds or carrots, throughout the day. I always took a walk outside in the afternoon. Then I'd repeat the process day in and day out.

Slowly, day by day, breath by breath, progress was made. Two steps forward, one back, two forward, two back, two forward, one back. Every day, words poured from my heart like these:

Thankful For My Heart

I love my heart
Heart beats in rhythm
Heart leads us our way
Listen to your heart
Heart is your intuition
My Life is a Path of Heart

Thankful For Forgiveness

Forgiveness Sets Us Free
Forgiveness is a Teacher
Forgiveness is Love
We need to Forgive Ourselves
We need to Forgive Others
Forgiveness is an Act of Surrendering
God Forgives
Forgive, Forgive, Forgive

Love Yourself

Love Yourself
Know Yourself
Be Yourself
Bring Yourself to the World

Lost
I'm lost
Don't know what to do, where to go
I'm scared
What steps to take
Help me find my way

Humble Man
The lessons of life have humbled me.
Life has opened my heart.
In order for it to be opened it had to be crushed
Hearts cannot be broken, only egos can
As I look out my window I see gray and rain, but look at it with
    new eyes.
How grateful and thankful for today
Live in the present
Spread love and light today
A Humble Man

On Christmas morning I woke up in my apartment alone. I missed not having my girls, and my dog. Still, I knew that, despite this, I wasn't alone at all. So, I sang "Happy Birthday" to Jesus. Then I sprung out of bed and made some coffee.

Before picking up my rosary beads, I said, "God, I'm lost. What I am supposed to do?"

"Write!" It was a thunderous message; my body shook.

I replied, "Write what?" No response.

That was the moment the words, "book, radio show, and website with blog" that I'd referenced in the Introduction came forth. It sparked me to open all my journals, and I sprawled them out all over the bed. I picked one up, then another and another. Reading them, I thought of all the obstacles that I'd overcome, including that time almost 20 years ago to the exact date when I'd contemplated taking my own life. That was the same day I'd brought God fully into my life.

One day, I felt filled with a huge amount of gratitude for my whole life as I walked back to my apartment after a great yoga workout. When I entered the apartment, I wrote down these words: *"The Humble Warrior Book."*

It suddenly occurred to me that "radio" meant podcast, *The Humble Warrior* Podcast, and the blog would be *The Humble Warrior* blog. Armed with my pile of journals, I thought about writing *The Humble Warrior* book, but I didn't have a clue as to how to write a book.

So, I went over to my bookshelf and looked at all the books I'd read over the years. Since many were published by Hay House, I pulled up the Hay House website and signed up for their writer's workshop and their "Speak, Write, and Promote" workshop a few months later. I also signed up for a 3-day "Warrior Training" hosted by an organization called, The Mankind Project, as well as a very unique yoga system offered by Jonny Kest at the Center for Yoga in Birmingham, MI. I felt that, with what I practiced on a daily basis and having participated in these events, I would be in a much better place when I actually started to write my book.

This idea turned out to be true. Between the Hay House workshops, and my journey into Jonny Kest's yoga system, my body-mind-spirit connection blossomed like never before. Yoga drew my attention inwards and kept me connected with God. As I moved through each pose, and breathed deeply, I felt closest to God and connected to all in the Universe.

I discovered that yoga is no longer a woman's game. I met many awesome warriors to connect with through yoga, and men continue to join it by leaps and bounds.

For me, yoga and meditation were the last components necessary to create the perfect spiritual fitness practice. Yoga taught me vulnerability. Yoga doesn't soften you; it strengthens you. Yoga brought out the best in me. It taught me and it humbled me. Another benefit was that I got to be part of a yoga community, which supercharged my growth.

CHAPTER 13

Forgiving Sets Us Free

Forgiveness doesn't happen overnight, it takes time. I had to first come to a place of forgiving myself for the end of our marriage before I could start the process of forgiving my former wife. So I did my daily spiritual fitness routine of prayer, rosary, nutrition, yoga, reading, journaling, and meditating. My relationship with God comforted me along the way.

As I worked on forgiving myself, I finally came to a place where I wanted to forgive my former wife, but how?

Then the day arrived...

I'd signed up for a conference in San Diego and booked my flight to the west coast. Since the event date fell on my weekend to watch our girls, I didn't think it would really be a problem to trade off for another weekend with my former wife. But guess what? She couldn't watch them because she and her new boyfriend had also booked a trip to San Diego that weekend – on the same flight as mine!

There are no coincidences in life. This is a Humble Warrior principle, so take this to heart. Everything is being orchestrated by something much greater than us, whether we can see the overall picture or not at any given time.

I told my former wife I would like to meet with her and her boyfriend in San Diego the night before my conference started.

By this time, we had been divorced close to 1½ years, and she was in the beginning process of introducing our three daughters to her new boyfriend. What mattered the most to me was to have the chance to speak my truth about how I felt regarding their situation, and more importantly, to forgive myself and my former wife.

I realized that I was a loving man connected to all. A spiritual warrior. And I looked forward to the chance to put this understanding to work.

†

*The Humble Warrior Golden Rule- I take
full responsibility for my life.
I don't blame anyone or anything for my
circumstances. I create what I want in this life.*

†

Please refer to this Golden Rule as you read about our meeting. I don't blame my former wife for anything.

†

Spiritual Fitness in Action

I arrived at the hotel around noon, Pacific Time, and ate a healthy lunch. A few hours later, I took my 4.5 mile run, at a 7-minute-mile clip, because I wanted to sweat out any toxins. After that, I did some yoga postures before cooling down in an icy shower.

(It is healing for the body to switch temperatures like that and also helps with detoxing).

The meeting with my former wife and her boyfriend was to take place at 6 PM. Refreshed and centered, I headed for our table at 5:30, which gave me a half hour to enjoy a view of the beautiful Pacific out the window in the restaurant.

During this time, I thanked God for my relationship with my former wife. I thanked Him for teaching me the art of forgiveness. It felt like everything was coming full circle for me in that moment. An intention's plan I'd written out on Christmas Day was working. The plan had stated that I would maintain my daily spiritual fitness routine of prayer, rosary, nutrition, yoga, reading, journaling, and meditating.

Many times I'd cried through the Rosary, and a few times I'd cried on the yoga mat. My tears helped me to love myself unconditionally. Through prayer, yoga, meditation, writing, and God's love, I was able to finally and truly forgive myself for all the mistakes I had made that had contributed to the breakdown of our marriage. I was learning compassion and kindness. And I was learning how to forgive my former wife for the ways I had felt hurt by her, too.

At five minutes to six, I prayed: "God, be with me now." Then I closed my eyes and listened to the gentle, lulling sound of the sea.

By the time they arrived, I was totally prepared. When I approached her boyfriend, I gave him a hug.

"All is cool, my brother."

Then we sat down and I looked into my former wife's eyes. I wanted to make sure my forgiveness was genuine. We'd had many disagreements, for example, over the timing of when our children would be introduced to her boyfriend's family, and other issues of that nature. So, I spoke my truth to her about my thoughts. Knowing that it was important for me to speak my truth, I accepted that whatever they did from there on with regard to introducing their kids to each other would be out of my control.

††

Whatever is going to happen will be. I have inner peace. This is the art of surrendering.

††

The meeting lasted only 20 minutes, and at the end, I wished them the best. I gave the boyfriend a few tips as to how to approach my former wife's father, built that connection bridge, and wished them the best on their journey. When they left I stared out at the ocean once more, and again, gave thanks for my time with her.

††

I offer my experience to those of you who struggle in your own relationships. You can do the physical, emotional, mental, and spiritual work to find the root cause. You can come to peace and the acceptance of your pain.

††

It felt so good to truly forgive. I was ready to let go and move on.

The following morning, I was well-rested in time for the conference, and I was ready for whatever might unfold. The first order of business was the introduction of an exercise in which we had to write about a defining moment in our lives from another's perspective. I was amazed to go within and see that the "other" I wanted to write in the voice of was none other than God, Himself!

I closed my eyes, took a deep breath and asked God what He wanted to say to me. My hand began to shake and tears dropped on the pages...

"*My boy, it's time. You are no longer a boy; you are a man who needs to teach. Teach what I have taught you. Tell them the Love I have for them. Tell them the Power that each one has. Teach Me like I have never been taught. Speak from the Heart. I'm with you...*"

As part of the exercise, we were also to break down our entire life's purpose into one defining sentence. I received clarity on that one defining sentence that summed up my whole life, and it will anchor me to my life force for the rest of my days: "It's in the heart where God speaks."

PART 2

Principles of a Humble Warrior: Spiritual Fitness Tools

The Humble Warrior is the book I wish I'd had when I was going through my divorce. It doesn't need to take twenty years and a bunch of rock bottom moments (though these are wakeup calls) to make a change or to rediscover your true self. All you have to do is claim, "I want change!" and then take action steps to do it.

Start now. Say, "I want change!" You're already on your way. The tools I am about to share with you will work. They will help you right now if you're going through a tough time and are looking to live a life of purpose.

Before sharing the Spiritual Fitness tools, it's important to understand The Humble Warrior Way Principles, and take them to heart – where God speaks...

The Humble Warrior Way Principles

1) **Believe in You.** You have all the power within to make this change. The Universe wants you to have the most wonderful life possible. You are a gift to this world. Be grateful for your life and for all of your experiences.

2) **Commit to changing, but do not judge yourself.** Take action and also go with the flow. The Humble Warrior Lifestyle is a lifetime practice. Take your time.

3) **God/Universe has your back.** This is a spiritual practice, not a religious one. Whatever your belief system, know that this backing is in place for you. Stay awake and alert and you will be guided.

4) **Take full responsibility for your life.** Don't blame or point fingers at anyone if things are not going your way.

5) **We are all connected.** Anything with a heartbeat – including that fly you want to swat – is a part of the cosmic web of life. By making this simple mindset change of knowing everyone/everything is connected, your life will be better, guaranteed. Try it and find out.

6) **When someone does something hurtful to you, it has nothing to do with you.** You are not responsible for other peoples' actions or behaviors. Just do your part to keep your own side of the street clean.

7) **Your mission in every decision you make is to choose Love over Fear.** The same goes for all of your responses. This is a tough one, so keep working on it.

8) **Love yourself unconditionally.** Loving yourself unconditionally is the greatest gift you can give to yourself, your family, your friends, strangers, the world, and even the Universe. Loving and caring for yourself positively affects every being who comes across your path.

9) **Cultivate writing, meditation, yoga, prayer, and the other practices that follow.** By implementing these practices on a daily basis, you are able to become a more disciplined human being, which cultivates good habits for body, mind and spirit. These practices can help you connect to yourself, others and your highest self.

10) **Listen with your heart to hear the Voice of God.** *It's in the heart where God speaks.* My purpose lies within my heart, and is the internal Voice that keeps me connected to All That Is. Listen to your heart and stay connected to your internal guidance system – your Voice within. Your purpose lies within you. I am the purpose. And so are you.

Daily Spiritual Fitness Tools

The Humble Warrior Way is a daily spiritual fitness practice that consists of prayer, meditation, affirmations, eating the right foods/liquids, exercise, and reading. If you are fully committed to this way of life, in less than one year you will change your life for the better, big time. By implementing this practice – even if you do only one thing – you will be healthier, more loving and feel more humility overall. You will be more confident in yourself, and you will have learned how to listen to your heart. When you do, trust it and act on it.

1) Prayer

Every morning when I wake up and every evening before I go to bed I say this simple prayer: "God, thank you for today, I'm grateful for my life and this journey. I love you. How can I serve?"

Before every meal: "Thank you, God, for this food. May it give me the proper nourishment I need."

Before every workout: "Thank you, God, for my beautiful body."

After every workout: "Thank you, God, for this workout. Thank you for a healthy heart."

You can use my simple prayers or create your own prayers. These little prayers take less than ten seconds. They will deposit love and gratitude into your mind, over and over, that will pay dividends in the long run.

2) The Rosary

The Rosary, or any other type of prayer beads, can be another way to access your daily dose(s) of godliness. The daily Rosary is at the core of my practice, even though I do not consider myself a religious person. The Rosary is my commitment to myself and to God. It keeps me awake. Doing the Rosary sometimes turns into a prayer, a meditation, a conversation with God, or I just simply go through the rote practice of it. The main point is that it's a commitment in which you plant your daily thoughts of God in your mind, heart, and spirit.

Sometimes, I do the Rosary in 10 minutes, while other times it requires 20, 30, or even 60 minutes. It depends on what I need at the time, and where my heart is leading me. For example, when I was going through my divorce, these sessions would last much longer, until I felt comfort in my heart.

Go to www.RosaryCenter.org if you would like instructions as to how to do the Rosary. Find what works for you. The Rosary, or any other form of prayer, should be effortless and not feel like a burden. You can start by doing the Rosary once a week and build up from there. If performing the Rosary doesn't resonate with you, please substitute it with something that works best for you, or sit in quiet meditation.

3) Nutrition

Paying attention to the nutritional needs of the body has to be done daily. You need to nourish your body. Start taking care of your body – this is a must. Do not expect to have a healthy body or spirit unless you make your body a priority – bottom line. By eating healthy and drinking the right liquids you are taking care of the body that houses your spirit, soul, mind, and heart.

Drink filtered water with electrolytes if you can. Some people say to drink 4 to 8 oz. an hour. What's worked well for me is 100 oz. per day. You could also invest in a home water filter system. At night, keep a 12 oz. glass of water next to you, and when you wake up, after your prayer, drink that glass of water to start your morning.

Taking care of your body is the same as taking care of a piece of God. Give daily thanks before you eat. By giving thanks, your motivation to put the right stuff in your body will increase.

4) Yoga/Fitness/Exercise

Physical fitness needs to be practiced daily. You need to move your body. There is a reason the order is Body, Mind and Spirit. It's in this order that you need to approach your spiritual health. At a minimum, carve out 20 minutes a day – even if it's a walk. Do something you love. Have fun with it. Be creative. Run. Swim. Do Crossfit. Kickbox. Dance. Play sports.

5) Read

Reading is crucial for a path of spiritual fitness. Up until the age of 29, I didn't read anything except the sports page or the business section. That was the extent of my world. What I've found is that committing to read a little each day is the way to go. A spiritual warrior is one who reads anything to inspire himself. Personally, I like reading spiritual or personal development books, as well as biographies about entrepreneurs and athletes.

Daily readers in the morning have been a part of my routine for the past ten years. When you read something that's inspiring briefly at the start of your day, you can plant positive words in your head. I highly recommend starting with *Positive Thinking Every Day* by Norman Vincent Peale. If you're going through a tough time, I highly recommend *The Book of Awakening* by Mark Nepo. These two daily readers will take you less than three minutes to read.

Read books for 20 minutes a day before you go to bed as well, or as a substitute for television.

6) Write

Writing is a core component in the Spiritual Fitness practice. For a guy, it might seem a little intimidating or weird to keep a journal, but this is also a must. Journaling isn't something you need to do daily. To start, just take 10-20 minutes to write once a week. Don't think, just write. Let the pen hit the paper and go. Let it come from your heart, not your head. Writing is a gateway to the heart. Make the journal your best friend. Write your story.

7) Affirmations

At first, I thought saying an affirmation was kind of silly. Through experience and practice, however, I now know that they work and they only take about five seconds of your time a day. Affirmations are great mind training. By doing them, you can change certain patterns about your lifestyle.

I use a 365-day calendar that offers a single, positive affirmation for each day. I keep this calendar right by my coffee maker and read it after my gratitude prayer. In addition, I have my own personal affirmations that I repeat daily in the morning and throughout the day. One example is, I look in the mirror first thing in the morning, and say: "I'm well. I'm happy, I have peace within." Another affirmation I use throughout the day is, "I am love. I am everything."

8) Meditate

Meditate for 5 – 40 minutes per day. There are many different methods, and I continue to experiment with them. Be creative. Start with 5 minutes a day in stillness, preferably in the morning before breakfast, or alternatively, before dinner.

I currently do Transcendental Meditation, which takes 20 minutes before breakfast and another 20 minutes before dinner. More information about Transcendental Meditation can be explored at www.TM.org.

✝✝

Spiritual Fitness Template

Below is a sample template for a Spiritual Fitness routine for you to refer to.

6:00 AM – Prayer of Gratitude/Thanks. Glass of Water. Morning Affirmation. Read Daily Affirmation.

6:20 AM – 20 minute meditation.

6:45 AM – Rosary. Could last up to an hour if God and I are on a roll.

7:15 AM – Daily readers.

8:30 or 9:45 AM – Yoga class.

(Throughout the day, anytime you see yourself in a mirror, repeat your affirmation. Mine is: "I am love. I am everything.")

9:30 PM– Read 20 minutes.

10:00 PM – Nightly gratitude prayer. Lights out.

✝✝

This is the core of what I do every day for my spiritual practice. You can use this template as an example to create a spiritual practice that works for you, or create your own template. Don't feel overwhelmed. Take it day by day. This is a lifetime practice and lifestyle transition.

Spiritual Emergencies

1) Ask for help. Start with God/Universe, then find the right person to talk to. For example, first I prayed to God and asked for help and guidance, then I visited my sister. I called my friend Linda next, and I also had a few appointments with a therapist.

2) Start eating healthy/drinking healthy. Reduce or eliminate those substances that are your weaknesses or that knock you down flat – like alcohol and sugar.

3) Find a tribe/support group. For me, my tribe was at the yoga studio. Depending on the issues you're facing, you have choices. Know that you're not alone.

4) Implement writing and reading daily until you feel at ease. Eliminate outside distractions like TV. Work on your positive thinking.

5) Make GOD your best friend. Yep. Right now! All will be well.

6) Work on you. Focus on what you CAN change and have control over, right this very minute. I love you, Warrior.

††

Humble Warriors live a life of no regrets. If you have any regrets, or if you harbor emotions in relation to any issues that weigh heavily on your heart, resolve them through some sort of forgiveness ceremony. Be 100% honest. Start speaking the Truth – even when it hurts. We think we are protecting people by not telling the truth, but this is not the way that truth works. The truth is helpful as long as it comes from your heart. It can be hard to speak the truth, but once you do, and you master this, you will feel free. Be kind to yourself in the process.

It took me many years to make the Spiritual Lifestyle work for me. I had to let go of those things that didn't serve me – like television, fantasy football, overeating, abuse of alcohol, smoking, and negative people. I choose to be around people who see the glass as being half full, not as being half empty.

Claim: "I want change." Come to peace with your story. Engage in a daily spiritual fitness practice. Commit to living a purposeful life that will allow you to shine and share your light – the light of your True Self.

PART 3

Spiritual Fitness
Writing Exercises

Here are some writing exercises that you can use to jumpstart your Spiritually Fit writing routine.

Chapter 1 – Thoughts to Consider

In the first chapter I shared my story about the first time I heard "the Voice". Think back about your childhood. Did you ever have any type of "mystical" experience that happened to you when you were young that you thought was strange and that you didn't share with anyone? Have you ever heard a Voice within? Take 20 minutes to write about the above experience.

Chapter 2 – Thoughts to Consider

In the second chapter, I talk about not being good enough in my dad's eyes. Was there ever a time in your life when you didn't feel like you were good enough? Take 20 minutes to write about the above experience.

Chapter 3 – Thoughts to Consider

Was there a significant time in your life when you began, or stopped, exercising? At what age did you start exercising? Why did you start or stop? Take 20 minutes to write about your exercise routine.

Chapter 4 – Thoughts to Consider

In chapter four, I talk about not taking the keys away from my mother. Have you ever felt in your heart that you should do the right thing, but you made a different choice? Take 20 minutes to write about the above experience.

Chapter 5 – Thoughts to Consider

In this chapter, I share about the reality of a dream of me becoming a professional ball player not coming true. Do you have a dream that hasn't come true yet that is for your benefit? Take 20 minutes to write about the above experience.

Chapter 6 – Thoughts to Consider

In this chapter, I share my experiences with gambling and rock bottom moment. Was there a time in your life when you hit rock bottom? Take 20 minutes to write about the above experience.

Chapter 7 – Thoughts to Consider

In chapter seven, I share what I believe is the "American Dream." What does "Living the American Dream" mean to you? Take 20 minutes to write about the above experience.

Chapter 8 – Thoughts to Consider

In this chapter, I share two books that influenced my journey. Is there a book that has changed your life? Take 20 minutes to write about the above experience.

Chapter 9 – Thoughts to Consider

In this chapter, I share how I felt disconnected from God. Have you ever felt lonely or deserted by God? Take 20 minutes to write about the above experience.

Chapter 10 – Thoughts to Consider

Have you ever doubted your intuition? Take 20 minutes to write about the above experience.

Chapter 11 – Thoughts to Consider

In this chapter, I share my experience with the black-capped chickadee. Is there a certain animal that you resonate with? Do you believe you have a Spirit Animal? Take 20 minutes to write about the above experience.

Chapter 12 – Thoughts to Consider

Did a relationship end with someone who you loved deeply? How did that make you feel? Take 20 minutes to write about the above experience.

Chapter 13 – Thoughts to Consider

In this chapter, I share about the importance of forgiveness. Have you forgiven yourself for all mishaps, mistakes, betrayals, etc. that you have committed in your life? Take 20 minutes to write about the above experience.

Great job! You have cleansed yourself. Now it's time to forgive everyone who you believe has crossed you. You do not have to tell someone "I forgive you" in order for your forgiveness to be genuine. A Humble Warrior principle is that when you let your heart guide you, you will automatically act in alignment with your own truth. Forgiveness may take time. Through your writing, acknowledge and release anything painful that you've experienced. You have the power within to heal. Allow yourself to be transformed by putting your loving awareness and conscious attention on the issue at hand. Take 20 minutes to write about the above experience.

Conclusion

Heal. Grow. Share… *How beautiful God works.*

In writing this book, I followed the process that I was guided into on December 25, 2014. I wrote this book, *The Humble Warrior.* I co-host a podcast called, *The Humble Warrior podcast.* I created my website, wwwChrisForte.com, which features a blog.

In the beginning I didn't know what exact steps to take. I made a few wrong turns along the way, but here we are together. This is life. We all battle obstacles that are meant to help us grow. When a major storm happens that can turn your world upside down, it's difficult to comprehend that this situation might be for your highest good. All I know is that if I came through the other side in my experience, perhaps you can do it, too.

We all make mistakes in life. We all have problems. It's how we respond to these situations that make us who we are.

We are Spiritual Warriors who fight the good fight. We have the tools in our toolbox to take care of ourselves. We hold the awareness that living a spiritually fit life benefits our own personal growth process and enhances our spiritual growth evolution.

We are the Warriors who will continue to bring kindness, compassion, love, and enthusiasm to the world – despite all the outside noise. We all have great power within. And we will continue to train ourselves, for we know that there will be a time when we will need to share our light, which is the expression of who we are in the world and what we stand for. Through our growth, we can share our light, for that is our purpose. Our purpose is to be our most beautiful true self.

You are the Purpose. You were created to be You and to bring your spark of light into the world.

We are beautiful people who have God's backing at all times. It's important to understand that you have God's backing all the time as you go forth to heal, grow, and share your light in the world.

I'm very humbled, blessed and grateful to be able to share my story with you.

I wish you many blessings on your journey. There is only one you – and you are the BEST in the world. Live Brave.

✝✝

Live Brave, and Listen to your Heart.

Gratitudes

There aren't enough words that I could put on paper to express the gratitude I have for Jon Moises, my partner on *The Humbler Warrior podcast,* Sara Vos, my writing coach, and Kelsey Hogan, my friend who spent many hours by my side. In addition, I would like to thank my editor Randy Peyser who spent time, energy and poured love into completing this book.

Mom and Dad, you have been the perfect parents for me. You have always supported me in my nontraditional ways to navigate this world. It's truly a blessing we can celebrate this book together.

I would like to thank all the teachers and students at the Center for Yoga in Birmingham, MI. It was this community that helped me, through breath and movement every day, to stay focused and disciplined as I wrote this book.

I would like to thank Bob Roth of the David Lynch Foundation, and my teacher, James Cahaney, for the Transcendental Meditation technique, which was the perfect meditation practice for me to implement into my spiritual fitness lifestyle.

I would like to thank Linda Peterson Smith for all your teachings on holistic healing, and for all of the energy work you did on my three children and me. Thank you for being my teacher and friend.

My three daughters, Ava, Brooke and Simone – three of the strongest women on the planet. I'm blessed to have you three in my life. You're the BEST in the world.

JC, aka Jesus Christ. Thanks for being my friend, teacher and mentor. Each day, I'm working to emulate you and what you stood for – The Warrior of Warriors.

Creator/God – Thanks for not giving up on me… for always being in my corner. May I serve you in the way I was created – as my BEST Self.

To all my brothers and sisters on the Spiritual Warrior path, I'm forever grateful to march with you. *Live Brave.*

Made in the USA
Lexington, KY
11 June 2017